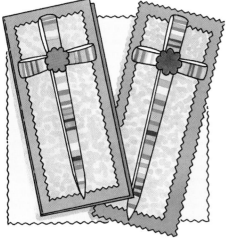

EASTER MAKE &DO

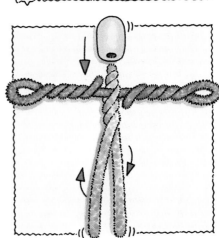

Gillian Chapman

Craft ideas which
bring the story of
Easter to life

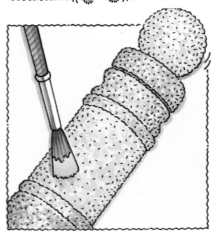

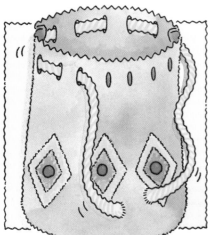

Resource Room
Church House
9 The Close
WINCHESTER
SO23 9LS
Tel: 01962 624760

HOW TO USE THIS BOOK

You will find within this book a wealth of ideas and inspiration for using with your child, group or Key Stage 2 classes.

Discover fresh ideas for Easter preparation and bring to life the New Testament accounts of the dramatic Easter story. And not a fluffy chicken in sight!

Craft ideas vary from the very simple to the more challenging, but the emphasis is strongly on using inexpensive materials and equipment, recycling and using domestic materials where possible. Children will experience the thrill of making something wonderful almost 'out of nothing'.

To help keep preparation time to a minimum, each project spread features:

✳ a lively retelling of the Bible story, suitable for reading aloud

✳ a list of materials needed

✳ clear step-by-step instructions

✳ a photograph of how the finished article may look, in case you haven't had time to make one earlier!

All the craft ideas have been designed, tried and tested by Gillian Chapman, a well-known author of craft books. Drawing on her wide experience of leading children's work-shops on arts and crafts, she has prepared a helpful section of Bible Craft Tips and safety recommendations. It is worth

taking a few moments to read through this section before you begin.

Part of the excitement and satisfaction of 'Make and Do' crafts begins when children are able to develop their own original slant on an idea or design, whatever the results! Some children (and adults, let's face it) may struggle to follow instructions and lose interest very quickly if they feel an activity is too difficult. Bearing that in mind, most of the ideas in this book can be modified according to a child's ability. For example, where sewing is involved, you may use PVA glue instead; where drawing is involved, you may cut pictures out of magazines.

You will find clear photocopiable tracing guides and templates in the middle of this book as a helpful starting-point. Some of these could be enlarged to produce wall-sized pictures, collages or displays for bedrooms, classrooms or churches.

Specific projects, such as the cup or the money-lenders' scales, could be used as props for drama productions. Having read the story and made the articles, children can enjoy the further dimension of bringing a story to life themselves through drama or dance. The Easter tableaux could also be used to re-enact the story.

There are endless possibilities for using 'Easter Make and Do' to explore the Bible. Enjoy them!

CONTENTS

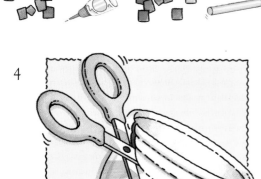

BIBLE CRAFT TIPS
Additional practical information

Safety First

All tools and equipment must be used with care and respect! Sharp pencils, scissors and needles can all be dangerous if used incorrectly.

However, an adult will need to help with carpentry tools and cutting tools.

If you need to use a craft knife make sure you also use a cutting board.

Paints

Poster paints are great for painting on paper and card, also to paint models made from paper pulp and papier mâché. They also come in metallic colours. Acrylic paints are better to paint wooden surfaces.

A jar of clean water will be needed to mix paints and to clean brushes. Change the water frequently to keep colours looking bright. Paints can be mixed on a palette or an old plate.

For detailed drawing of animals, figures and faces sketch in the outlines first with pencil, then colour in using coloured pencils. If you have a set of watercolour paints and a fine brush, use these.

Shaped Scissors

Special scissors with a shaped cutting blade are increasingly available for craftwork. Use these, or pinking shears, to give paper and fabric a special patterned edge such as for the palm cross cards and the fish hanging.

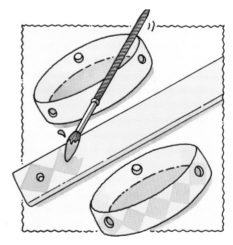

Glues

PVA glue is perfect for most craftwork. It can be diluted for papier mâché type projects. It will stick paper, card and most fabrics – but in most cases it must be used very sparingly. It will wash off with cold water.

Glue sticks are better for neat finishes, but only work on paper and thin card.

When using PVA to do fine work such as gluing beads and sequins on to fabric, try to buy the glue in a bottle with a fine nozzle. If you don't have such a container, then pour some of the glue into a small plastic container (like a lid) and use a cocktail stick to put tiny blobs of glue where it's needed.

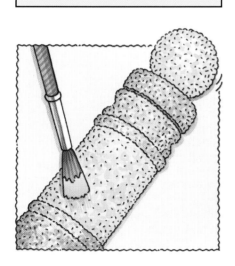

Keeping Clean

Make sure all work surfaces are protected with newspaper and all clothing is covered with overalls (e.g. an old shirt) or an apron. Keep an old towel handy for drying not-so-clean hands.

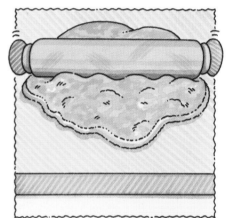

Brushes

Keep separate brushes for painting and gluing. Always clean them in warm soapy water after use and dry them before putting them away.

JESUS ENTERS JERUSALEM

Here comes the King!

Jesus and his friends were going to Jerusalem for the Passover festival.

Jesus sent two of his friends on ahead, saying, 'Go to the village over there where you will find a young donkey. Bring it to me. Say that your master needs it.'

The two friends found the donkey, put their cloaks over the donkey's back and brought it to Jesus.

Jesus rode into the great city of Jerusalem.

Huge crowds came to greet Jesus, spreading their cloaks on the road and waving palm branches.

'Hosanna!' they shouted.

They cheered and waved to Jesus, their King, who came to Jerusalem riding on a donkey.

You will need:

A4 sheets of thin coloured card

Scraps of coloured paper

Pieces of coloured wrapping paper

Scissors

Glue stick

Ruler and pencil

Shaped scissors or pinking shears

Coloured shaped stickers, over 2cm in size: hearts, stars, circles

Make these palm crosses to remember how the crowds cheered for Jesus.

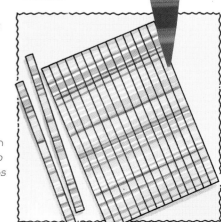

1 Measure and mark strips 2cm wide by 40cm long on the wrapping paper. You will need two strips for each cross. Carefully cut out the strips using the scissors.

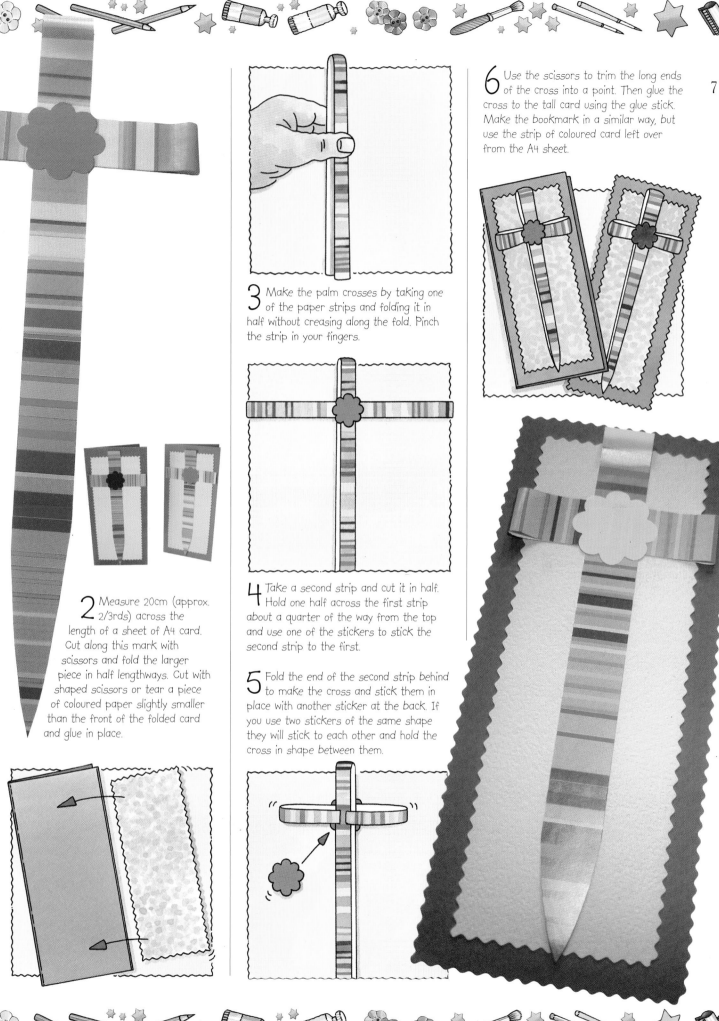

6 Use the scissors to trim the long ends of the cross into a point. Then glue the cross to the tall card using the glue stick. Make the bookmark in a similar way, but use the strip of coloured card left over from the A4 sheet.

3 Make the palm crosses by taking one of the paper strips and folding it in half without creasing along the fold. Pinch the strip in your fingers.

4 Take a second strip and cut it in half. Hold one half across the first strip about a quarter of the way from the top and use one of the stickers to stick the second strip to the first.

5 Fold the end of the second strip behind to make the cross and stick them in place with another sticker at the back. If you use two stickers of the same shape they will stick to each other and hold the cross in shape between them.

2 Measure 20cm (approx. 2/3rds) across the length of a sheet of A4 card. Cut along this mark with scissors and fold the larger piece in half lengthways. Cut with shaped scissors or tear a piece of coloured paper slightly smaller than the front of the folded card and glue in place.

JESUS CLEARS THE TEMPLE

Jesus is angry!

When Jesus arrived in Jerusalem, he set off towards the Temple. He wanted to pray to God in the holy place of this noisy, bustling city. But when Jesus entered the Temple area, he saw something which made him very angry indeed. There were people buying and selling animals and doves, and other people were changing money. The whole place had become a noisy, smelly market place, just like the rest of the city.

Jesus turned over the tables with a great crash. The doves flew away. The people behind the tables were shocked. What was Jesus doing?

You will need:

A small round box
e.g. empty cheese box

Scissors
(and some adult help)

Ruler

24cm x 4cm
balsa wood strip

Poster paints
and brush

7 x 35cm
lengths of string

Large blunt needle

3 x large
wooden beads

1 Ask an adult to help you make three holes an equal distance apart from each other in the rims of the lid and base of the round box, using the sharp point of the scissors.

2 Using the ruler to position them accurately, ask an adult to help you make three holes in the balsa wood strip, again using the point of the scissors. Make a hole exactly in the centre of the strip and one hole 2cm from either end.

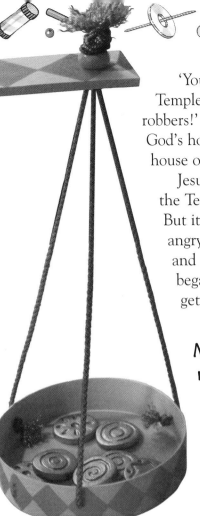

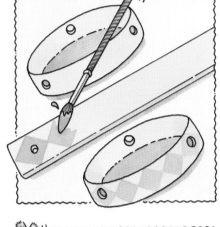

'You are turning the Temple into a den of robbers!' shouted Jesus. 'It is God's house. It should be a house of prayer!'

Jesus wanted to keep the Temple a holy place. But it made many people angry. The chief priests and teachers of the law began to make plans to get rid of Jesus.

Make these money-lenders' scales like the ones used in the Temple courts.

3 Use the poster paints to paint the lid and base of the box and the balsa wood strip. Money-lenders' scales would have been made from metal, but you can paint your scales with bright patterns.

4 Thread a length of string through each of the three holes in the lid of the box and tie a knot at the end of each string. Use the large blunt needle to thread the three lengths through the hole in the end of the strip and through a bead, then tie the three ends together.

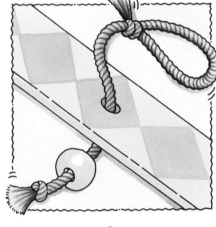

5 Repeat these instructions and attach the base of the card box to the other end of the strip in the same way. Thread the needle with the last piece of string and tie a knot in the end of the string. Thread it through a bead, then through the centre hole and tie a loop in the end.

6 If you have measured and made your scales accurately, they should be evenly balanced when you hold them up by the central string. Use small coins as weights and use your scales to weigh out sweets or small pieces of fruit and nuts.

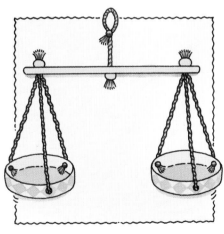

MARY'S GIFT TO JESUS

The smell of perfume fills the room

Shortly before Passover, Jesus went to eat at a friend's house. A woman called Mary came up to Jesus, holding a small but very precious alabaster jar.

When Mary opened the jar, the sweet smell of perfume wafted out. Mary had brought a very expensive gift for Jesus. She poured it over his head.

'What's she doing?' asked some of Jesus' friends. 'That's a real waste of money, just pouring it away like that!'

Jesus heard them complaining and said quietly, 'Leave her alone. She has shown how much she loves me. She has done a beautiful thing.'

You will need:

✂

Small glass jar with screw top lid, e.g. herb or spice jar

Paper kitchen towel

Small plastic ping-pong ball

PVA glue and brush

Poster paints and brush

Metallic poster paints

Small beads, needle and thread for decoration

Remove the lid from the clean glass jar and brush an area of the surface with PVA glue. Tear up small pieces of kitchen towel and stick them to the surface but avoid gluing the paper to the screw top rim.

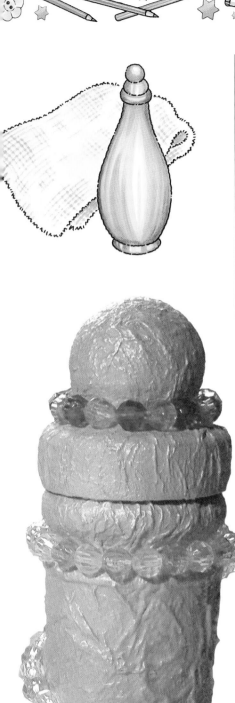

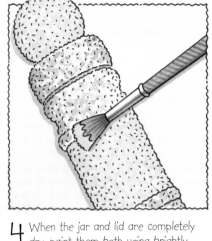

2 Continue to cover the surface of the jar, making sure that the paper remains crinkly. Cover the lid, keeping it separate from the jar. Leave to dry and then add more layers to give an extra crinkly texture to the surface.

4 When the jar and lid are completely dry, paint them both using brightly coloured poster paints. The perfume jar that Mary used was made of alabaster and would have looked very plain, but you can decorate your perfume jar to make it look very special. Leave to dry.

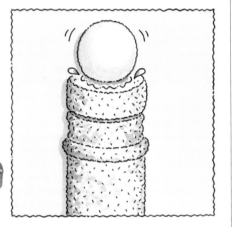

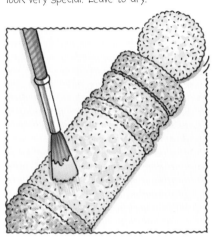

3 Glue the plastic ball to the top of the lid and cover it with the glued kitchen paper so it has a crinkly texture to match the jar.

5 To make the jar look very expensive, brush a thin coat of gold or silver paint sparingly over the surface, making sure the first colour still shows through.

Make this jar to remind you of Mary's gift to Jesus.

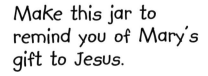

6 Finally, decorate the perfume jar. Thread very small beads on to a length of thread and tie the ends firmly. Wind the thread of beads around the jar and glue them firmly in place.

THIRTY PIECES OF SILVER

Judas becomes a traitor

The chief priests wanted to get rid of Jesus. But they didn't know how to capture him.

Judas Iscariot, who had been one of Jesus' closest friends, was greedy for money. He thought of a plan to get rich quick.

Judas went to the chief priests and asked, 'What will you pay me if I hand Jesus over to you?'

'We'll give you thirty pieces of silver,' they said.

'Done!' said Judas.

Judas watched for a chance to hand Jesus over to them. He was no longer a friend of Jesus. He was his enemy.

You will need:

TO MAKE THE COINS

Self-hardening clay

Rolling pin and wooden or plastic board

Small cocktail sticks, pencils and carving tools

Round plastic bottle top

Sheets of paper kitchen towel

Silver poster paint and brush

TO MAKE THE MONEY BAG

15cm x 30cm piece of felt

Needle, thread and scissors

40cm length of cord

Scraps of felt and beads

1 Using the rolling pin, roll out the clay on the board to an even thickness of about 0.5cm.

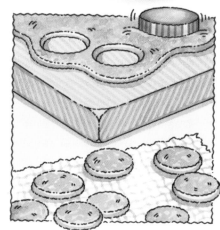

2 Use the round plastic lid as a cutter to cut out 30 circular shapes from the clay. Carefully remove these clay circles from the board and place them on the kitchen towel.

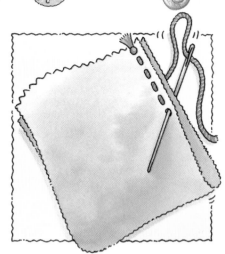

5 Coins were often kept safe in small money bags made from leather or cloth. To make the bag, fold the rectangle of felt in half and sew along two sides using a small simple running stitch.

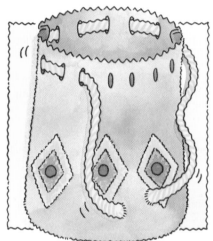

Make these silver coins as a reminder of how Judas turned against Jesus.

6 Turn the bag inside out so the stitching is on the inside. Decorate the bag by gluing on scraps of felt and beads. Ask an adult to make a line of small holes about 2cm from the opening with the scissors. Thread the cord in and out of the holes. Thread a small bead on to each end and secure with a knot. Fray the ends then tie the ends together. Keep your silver coins in the money bag and pull the cord tight to keep them safe.

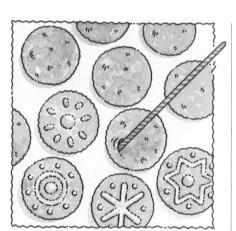

3 Use the small sticks and tools to decorate the clay circles, making them look like coins. Roman coins were often decorated with the head of the emperor, but you can think of your own designs. Try to keep the coins flat and leave the clay to dry out completely.

4 When the clay coins are dry, use the poster paint to paint them silver. Paint one side and leave to dry before turning over to paint the reverse side.

JESUS WASHES HIS FRIENDS' FEET

Jesus shows his friends how much he loves them

Jesus knew that he would not be with his friends for much longer. He wanted to celebrate the Passover meal with them one last time. It was a special time of remembering how God had rescued Moses and the Israelites from slavery in Egypt many years ago.

Jesus met his twelve friends at the upper room of a house in Jerusalem.

Jesus took a bowl of water and began to wash his friends' feet.

'You mustn't wash my feet!' said Peter. 'You are our master, not our servant!'

'Unless I wash you, you don't belong to me,' said Jesus.

'Then wash my hands and head as well!' said Peter.

Jesus washed Peter's feet.

'Now that I have washed your feet,' said Jesus, 'you must also wash each other's feet. Do as I have done.'

You will need:

✂

Large round plastic bowl

Newspaper

PVA glue and brush

Cling film
and cooking oil

Light brown poster paint
and brush

Scissors

Coloured pages
from magazines

Pencil

Varnish (optional)

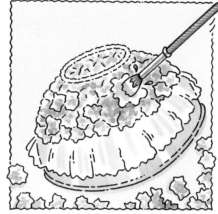

1 Use the round plastic bowl as your mould. Lightly grease the outside with the oil and cover with the cling film. Cover the outside of the bowl with six layers of newspaper pieces glued with diluted PVA. The design of this papier mâché bowl is fairly shallow so you will only need to cover about 20cm up the sides.

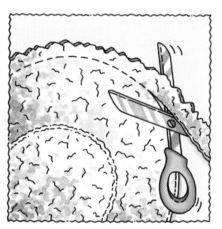

2 Leave the papier mâché to dry overnight, then remove it from the plastic bowl by pulling away the cling film. Neaten the papier mâché bowl by trimming around the edges with the scissors.

3 Neaten the edge of the bowl further by gluing small strips of glued newspaper around the rim. Leave to dry.

4 When it is dry, paint the bowl inside and out with a light brown colour to make the bowl look as if it is made from clay. Decorate the bowl with a simple mosaic pattern. Draw the outline in pencil around the rim of the bowl and include a small design in the centre.

5 Cut out lots of small squares from the coloured pages of magazines and arrange all the squares into groups of similar colours to make the mosaics. This design does not cover the bowl completely, but makes a border pattern and central design.

6 Follow the pencil guide lines and glue the coloured squares to the surface of the bowl with PVA. Build up the mosaic pattern and overlap the squares if necessary. When you have finished decorating the bowl, you could varnish it to help strengthen and protect the mosaic.

Make this mosaic bowl and think about how much Jesus loved his friends.

TABLEAU FIGURES

You will need:

✂

TO MAKE THE FIGURES

Craft pipe cleaners

Scissors

Scraps of coloured
fabric, felt and yarns

Wooden beads
for heads

Thin black felt
tipped pen

Rolls of thin card

Sticky tape

Paper kitchen towel

PVA glue
and glue brush

Paints and brush

Cocktail sticks

TO MAKE THE SWORDS, CLUBS AND TORCHES

Scraps of grey/silver
card

Paper kitchen towel

Paints and brush

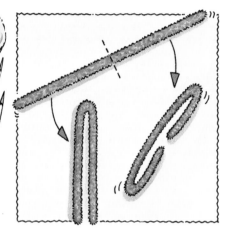

1 Make the basic structure of all the figures by bending and twisting two pipe cleaners as shown.

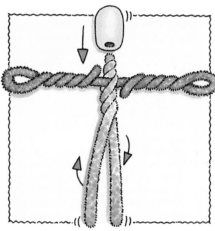

2 Stick a bead on top as a 'head'. Wrap the 'arms' with coloured yarn.

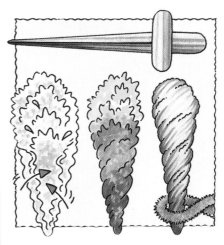

3 Glue the pipe cleaners into a rolled up piece of thin card 6cm wide to make them stable. Secure with tape. Draw the face features on to the bead using the black felt tipped pen.

4 Dress the figures in different coloured fabric. Fit a long piece over the head and tie in place around the waist. Glue a triangular shape to the head to make a headdress. Use a cocktail stick to dab tiny blobs of PVA where needed.

Some of the figures hold swords, clubs, torches and sticks. Make the swords by cutting out small pieces of silver card and glueing together. Make the torches and clubs by twisting pieces of glued kitchen paper towel together and moulding to make the shapes. Then paint them. Attach the weapons and sticks by pushing them through the pipe cleaner loops at the ends of the arms.

TABLEAU FIGURES

 JESUS DIES ON A CROSS
Pages 26-27

 JESUS IS ALIVE!
Pages 28-29

For the Roman soldier, thread two button feet on to the pipe cleaner legs. Tie felt grieves around his legs and attach a felt cloak across his body. Make his helmet from small pieces of kitchen foil shaped to fit the bead head. Add spear as shown.

You will need:

TO MAKE THE SOLDIER
2 x large buttons
Scraps of foil
Scraps of felt
Cocktail stick

TO MAKE THE ANGEL
1 x large button
Brown and yellow yarn
Scraps of grey/silver card
Scraps of white fabric

TO MAKE THE GRAVE CLOTHES
Paper kitchen towel
Scraps of white fabric

To give the angels a seated shape, thread a button through the pipe cleaner legs as shown. Make their hair from lengths of brown yarn glued across the bead head.

Cut out wings from silver card (see template) and attach to the back of the figure with a length of yellow yarn. Dress the angels with garments made from white fabric.

The grave clothes were left in the tomb when Jesus rose from the dead. Make the body shroud from lengths of glued kitchen towel, wrapped to make a cocoon shape. The head cloth is a piece of white fabric folded together.

TRACING GUIDES

JESUS DIES
ON A CROSS
Pages 26-27

BREAKFAST ON
THE BEACH
Pages 30-31

THE LAST SUPPER
Jesus shares a special meal with his friends

After Jesus had finished washing everyone's feet, he reclined at the table with his friends, ready to eat the Passover meal of roasted lamb, bread without yeast, bitter herbs and wine.

Jesus looked at his friends gathered around him.

You will need:

✂

2 x clean plastic dessert pots

Plastic cotton reel

Scissors

String, split peas and lentils

Paper kitchen towel

Sticky tape

PVA glue and brush

Cocktail stick

Silver or brown poster paint

Paint brush

Make this special cup to remember Jesus' words at the Last Supper.

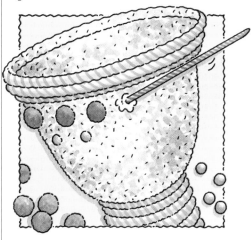

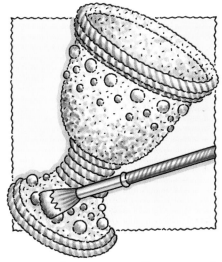

'One of you is going to hand me over to be killed,' he said.
His friends were very worried.

'Surely not I!' each one said to another.

Jesus already knew it would be Judas Iscariot.

While they were eating, Jesus took the bread, broke it
and gave it to his friends.

'Eat this and remember me,' said Jesus. 'This is my body.'

Then he took the cup of wine, thanked God for it, and
handed it round.

'Drink this and remember me,' said Jesus. 'This is my blood, given for many.'

Jesus' friends drank the wine.
They sang a song together, then
went out to the Mount of
Olives.

1 Use the scissors carefully to cut out the
bottom section of one of the dessert
pots to form the base of the cup. Tip this
upside-down, as shown here. The cotton
reel will form the stem of the cup.

2 Use the PVA to glue the cotton reel
between the two pots and leave to dry.

3 Brush the surface with PVA glue and
begin to cover the pots with torn pieces
of paper towel. The layers of paper towel
will help to hold the two plastic pots and
the cotton reel together. Make sure the
paper remains nice and crinkly. Cover the
whole surface inside and out with at least
two layers of paper and leave to dry.

4 Wind a length of string around the rim
of the cup, fixing the string in place
with dabs of glue. Then glue string around
the stem and the base of the cup and
leave to dry.

5 Make a raised pattern on the surface
of the cup with split peas and lentils.
Place small blobs of PVA glue on the
surface using the cocktail stick and
carefully position the peas and lentils on the
glue.

6 When you have finished decorating the
cup, leave the glue to dry. Then paint
the cup inside and out with the silver or
brown poster paint. It is likely that the cup
Jesus used would have been made of
earthenware. Today the cups used in
churches tend to be made of silver.

24

THE GARDEN OF GETHSEMANE

Jesus is arrested

On the Mount of Olives was a garden called Gethsemane. Here Jesus knelt down to pray to God. He knew that the time was coming for him to be taken away.

Jesus asked his friends to pray with him. But they kept falling asleep.

'Why are you sleeping?' he asked them. 'Watch and pray with me.'

Suddenly a crowd of soldiers and others sent by the chief priests and Jewish leaders came towards them with torches, clubs and swords. Judas led the group and came up to Jesus to kiss him. This showed the soldiers where Jesus was.

One of Jesus' friends took out a sword and in his fear chopped off the ear of the high priest's servant.

'Put that sword away,' said Jesus. 'All who use the sword will die by the sword. Things must happen in this way.'

Then Jesus touched the servant's ear and healed it.

Jesus was then arrested and taken away to the high priest.

To assemble this tableau you will need Jesus, the disciples, Judas, the guards and onlookers, using the instructions on pages 16-19.

You will need:

✂

TO MAKE THE CARD TRAY AND BACKDROP

Corrugated card 40cm x 30cm for the tray

Pencil and scissors

Thick card 40cm x 25cm for the backdrop

Pair of compasses

Paper kitchen towel, PVA glue and glue brush

Poster paints and brush

Small pieces of greenery and foliage

Plasticine or florists' oasis

Sand and small pebbles or gravel

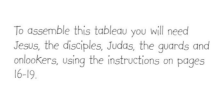

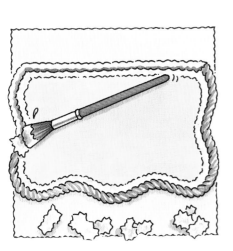

I Draw a random shape on the card, leaving the upper side straight and cut out the shape with the scissors. Glue a strip of crumpled newspaper around the edge of the card to form a ridge, then cover with pieces of glued kitchen towel. Leave to dry, then paint to resemble rocks and stones. Decorate with sand and small sized gravel, small pieces of greenery and foliage, pushed into plasticine or florists' oasis.

Make this tableau scene and recreate the drama in the Garden of Gethsemane.

2 Draw a semi-circular arch on the card with the compasses, then carefully cut it out. Paint it to reflect the atmosphere of the garden setting at night. Position the backdrop behind the scene base. Glue in place and prop it up with a suitable weight (e.g. a tin of soup).

3 To make the figures on this page turn to pages 16 to 19 for full instructions.

JESUS DIES ON A CROSS

The people shout, 'Crucify him!'

The soldiers who were guarding Jesus were very cruel to him. Jesus was brought before Pilate, the Roman governor.

'What has this man done wrong?' Pilate asked the crowd.

'He is causing trouble all over the country,' said the chief priests. 'He says he is a king.'

'Are you the King of the Jews?' asked Pilate.

'Yes, it is as you say,' said Jesus.

'What shall I do with Jesus?' Pilate asked the crowd.

'Crucify him!' they shouted. 'Put him on a cross to die!'

Pilate did not think Jesus had done anything wrong, but he wanted to please the crowd. So he handed Jesus over to the soldiers to be taken to a place called Golgotha. There he was nailed to a cross. Above his head was a sign saying: The King of the Jews.

It was a terrible day. Jesus' mother, Mary, stood close by and watched and wept.

At midday, darkness covered the land until the middle of the afternoon. Then Jesus cried out in a loud voice to God, and breathed his last breath.

You will need:

TO MAKE THE MOUND AND CROSSES

Newspaper

Sticky tape

Thick card for the crosses

Corrugated card for the base

Scissors

Paper kitchen towel

PVA glue and glue brush

Poster paints and brush

Sand and small pebbles or gravel

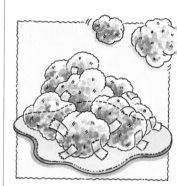

1 To make the figures (four women, weeping, two men and a Roman soldier) turn to pages 16 to 19 for full instructions.

2 First make a base for the mound by cutting out a random shape from the card with the scissors. Then crumple up balls of newspaper and tape them to the card base to make the basic height, form and shape of the mound. Tape all the balls of newspaper together to make a firm structure.

Make this dramatic tableau of the events of Good Friday.

3 Cover the newspaper structure with PVA glue. Take a square of kitchen towel, wet it under the tap, squeeze out the excess moisture and drape it over the newspaper, making sure it stays nice and crinkly. Cover the mound with more PVA and pieces of wet towel until all the newspaper is completely covered with the textured surface.

4 Leave to dry and then paint the mound to resemble a rock. Use a light brown paint to cover the surface then, when dry, brush over with grey paint to get a realistic effect.

5 Make the three crosses from strips of card, 8cm x 2cm and 15cm x 2cm, glued together with PVA, then painted. Use the template on page 20 to cut the figures from black felt and glue them to the crosses. Carefully use the tips of the scissors to make three slots in the mound and then slot the crosses into position.

6 Make or reuse the tray from page 24. Make a new backdrop and paint it with dramatic colours. Position the mound and crosses on the tray. Assemble the tableau as shown.

JESUS IS ALIVE!
God raises Jesus from death

Jesus' body was taken down from the cross and put in a borrowed tomb. A large stone was rolled in front to block the entrance.

Three days passed. All Jesus' friends were shocked. They didn't know what to do next.

Then, early on Sunday morning, some of the women went to his tomb with special spices to anoint his body. But what a shock they had when they got there! The large stone had been rolled away! Inside the tomb, Jesus' body had gone. All that was left was the strip of cloth that Jesus' body had been wrapped in, and the piece that was wrapped round his head was folded beside it.

Suddenly two angels in bright shining clothes appeared.

'Don't look for Jesus here,' they said. 'He's alive!'

The women couldn't believe it! They ran home at once and told Jesus' friends. Jesus was alive!

You will need:

TO MAKE THE TOMB

Small cardboard box (e.g. small shoe or pasta box)

Small rectangular box (e.g. toothpaste box)

Plastic circular lid or saucer, with a large enough diameter to cover tomb entrance

Newspaper

Sticky tape

Corrugated card for base

Scissors

Paper kitchen towel

PVA glue and glue brush

Poster paints and brush

Small pieces of greenery and foliage

Plasticine or florists' oasis

Sand and small pebbles or gravel

Make this Easter garden tableau and thank God for raising Jesus from death.

1 Draw an arch shape on one side of the larger box to represent the tomb entrance and cut it out. Glue the smaller box to the inside of the larger box to make the ledge inside the tomb.

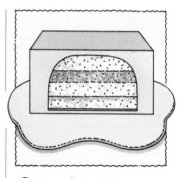

2 Cover all the inside surfaces of the box with glued pieces of kitchen roll to give a textured surface all over. Place the box on a piece of thick card and draw a shape around the box, leaving 10-12cm to the front and sides of the box. Cut out the shape and glue the box to the card.

3 Use crumpled balls of newspaper to build up the cave shape to the sides and top of the box. Hold the newspaper in place with sticky tape. Then using the same method described to make the mound on page 26, cover the newspaper with PVA glue and drape pieces of wet kitchen towel over the structure to make it look like a cave tomb.

4 Make a groove in front of the tomb for the stone to roll along. Build up the two sides of the groove with lengths of crumpled newspaper, held in place with pieces of glued kitchen towel.

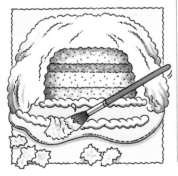

5 Make the rolling stone by covering the plastic lid with glued kitchen towel as described before. Paint the tomb and the rolling stone to look like rock.

7 Assemble the tableau using a tray and backdrop as shown on page 24. Paint the backdrop with golden rays. Use fresh foliage and pebbles to decorate the garden.

8 To make the figures (two women, two angels and Jesus) turn to pages 16 to 19 for full instructions.

BREAKFAST ON THE BEACH

Jesus appears to his disciples again

Over the next few days, Jesus appeared to his friends, showing them that he really was alive again.

One night, Peter and a group of disciples were out fishing in their boat. They had caught nothing. Early the next morning, Jesus stood on the shore, watching them. He was far away, so they couldn't see at first who it was.

'Haven't you caught any fish?' he shouted to the fishermen.

'No!' said Peter.

'Then throw your net on the other side of the boat,' said Jesus, 'and you will catch plenty!'

The men did as he said and sure enough, their nets were filled to bursting point with fresh, wriggling fish.

'It's Jesus!' said Peter. They knew that only Jesus could do something so amazing. Peter was so excited that he jumped out of the boat and swam to shore.

Jesus had made a small fire ready on the shore to cook some of the fish. He had some bread for them too. His friends came and sat with him and ate breakfast on the beach. It was wonderful to be with Jesus again!

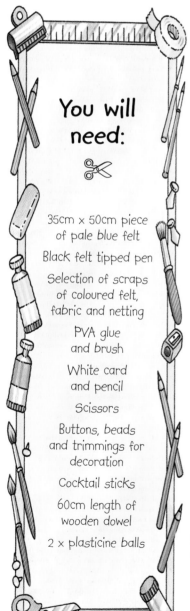

You will need:

✂

35cm x 50cm piece of pale blue felt

Black felt tipped pen

Selection of scraps of coloured felt, fabric and netting

PVA glue and brush

White card and pencil

Scissors

Buttons, beads and trimmings for decoration

Cocktail sticks

60cm length of wooden dowel

2 x plasticine balls

Draw one large and one small simple fish shape on the card. You could use the templates on pages 20-21. Cut the card shapes out carefully.

Make this wall hanging of the symbol of the fish, used by those who *believe* in Jesus.

5 Cut out two strips of fabric to fit along the two sides of the hanging and glue these in place. Then glue the small fish on top of these strips to make the border patterns. If you have any small buttons or beads, use them to decorate the fish.

2 Lay the card template on the fabric, draw around the shape with the felt tipped pen and cut it out. You will need two large fish and eight small ones. If you have a selection of fabrics, cut them out using different colours and patterns.

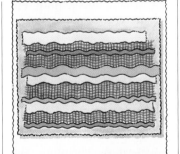

3 Cut out a number of wavy strips of coloured fabric and glue them across the background felt to make an underwater scene. Use blue, grey and green coloured netting and wavy trimmings. Don't worry about lining up the ends of the wavy strips along the two sides as these will be covered by the border pattern.

4 Glue the two large fish on to the centre of the scene, over the top of the waves. Cut out a number of fabric circles and glue these to the bodies of the fish to represent their scales.

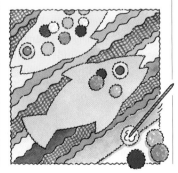

6 Cut out four strips of fabric to make loops along the top edge of the hanging and glue in place. Thread the wooden dowel through the loops and push a plasticine ball on each end to hold the hanging in place.

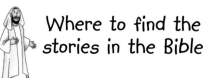

Where to find the stories in the Bible

Jesus enters Jerusalem:
Matthew 21:1-11; Mark 11:1-10;
Luke 19:29-38; John 12:12-15

Jesus clears the Temple:
Matthew 21:12-13; Mark 11:15-18; Luke 19:45-47

Mary's gift to Jesus:
Matthew 26:6-13; Mark 14:3-9

Thirty pieces of silver:
Matthew 26:14-16; Mark 14:10-11; Luke 22:3-6

Jesus washes his friends' feet:
John 13:1-17

The Last Supper:
Matthew 26:17-30; Mark 14:17-26; Luke 22:14-20

The garden of Gethsemane:
Matthew 26:36-56; Mark 14:32-50;
Luke 22:39-53

Jesus dies on a cross:
Matthew 27:11-50; Mark 15:1-38; Luke 23:33-46;
John 19:1-30

Jesus is alive!:
Matthew 27:57–28:10; Mark 16:1-8;
Luke 24:1-10

Breakfast on the beach:
John 21:1-14

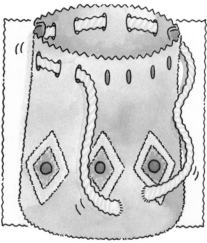

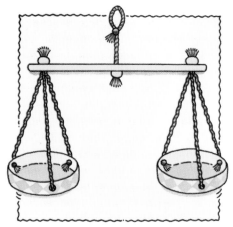

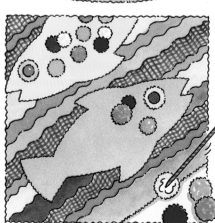

Published in the UK by
The Bible Reading Fellowship
First Floor, Elsfield Hall, 15-17 Elsfield Way, Oxford OX2 8FG
ISBN 1 84101 348 X

First edition 2004

Copyright © 2004 AD Publishing Services Ltd
1 Churchgates, The Wilderness, Berkhamsted, Herts HP4 2UB
Bible stories copyright © 2004 AD Publishing Services Ltd,
Leena Lane
Text and illustrations copyright © 2004 Gillian Chapman

Editorial Director Annette Reynolds
Project Editor Leena Lane
Art Director Gerald Rogers
Pre-production Krystyna Hewitt
Production John Laister

British Library Cataloguing in Publication Data.
A catalogue record for this book is available from
the British Library.

This material can be photocopied, duplicated or
enlarged for individual or group use.

Printed and bound in Singapore

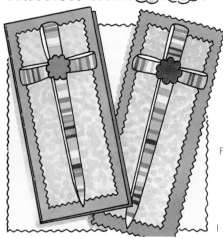